world writers
SUZANNE COLLINS

world writers
SUZANNE COLLINS

Kerrily Sapet

MORGAN
REYNOLDS
PUBLISHING

GREENSBORO, NORTH CAROLINA

TO THE FLYNNS,

May the odds be ever in your favor

Suzanne Collins

WORLD WRITERS SERIES

Suzanne Collins
Copyright © 2013 by Morgan Reynolds Publishing

Library of Congress Cataloging-in-
Publication Data

Sapet, Kerrily, 1972-
 Suzanne Collins / by Kerrily Sapet.
    p. cm. -- (World writers)
  ISBN 978-1-59935-346-3 -- ISBN 978-1-59935-347-0
(e-book) 1. Collins,
Suzanne. 2. Women authors, American--21st
century--Biography--Juvenile
literature. 3. Authors, American--21st
century--Biography--Juvenile
literature. I. Title.
 PS3603.O4558Z85 2012
 813'.6--dc23

                                          2012018324

Printed in the United States of America
First Edition

Book cover and interior designed by:
Ed Morgan, navyblue design studio
Greensboro, NC

TABLE OF CONTENTS

1

A Soldier's Daughter

As a young girl growing up in Belgium, Suzanne Collins toured old stone castles, visited other European countries, and stood in fields of vivid red poppies. Her father taught her to look beyond the "fairy-tale magical." The massive castles once stood as fortresses against invaders. The meadows of crimson flowers, that reminded her of a scene from *The Wizard of Oz*, were World War I battlefields. The poppies blanketing the graves of fallen soldiers had grown from seeds churned up and spread during artillery shelling. As an adult, Collins shaped these memories into stories involving war, violence, and children. Her dark tales have captivated people young and old around the world.

Suzanne Collins was born on August 10, 1962, in Hartford, Connecticut. Her parents, Michael and Jane Collins, had three older children: Kathy, Jeanie, and Drew. A career officer in the U.S. Air Force, Michael Collins was a military specialist, historian, and doctor of political science. Suzanne inherited her father's fascination with history and her mother's love of books.

Suzanne's father taught military history at the United States Military Academy at West Point. A national landmark, West Point is located just north of New York City, overlooking the Hudson River. Historic gray and black granite buildings dot the manicured green lawns. The 4,400 students, called cadets, are U.S. Army officers in training. One of Suzanne's earliest memories is of watching rows of young men in crisp uniforms drilling at West Point.

When Suzanne was six years old, her family moved to Indiana. Soon after, her father left to fight in the Vietnam War. Suzanne's family had a long history of serving their country. Called to battle in World War I, her grandfather was among the countless soldiers gassed by German troops. World War I had marked the first widespread use of gas as a weapon—from tear gas to blister-causing mustard gas to poisonous chlorine gas. During World War II, her uncle had sustained shrapnel wounds.

Graduates toss their hats during commencement
ceremonies at the United States Military Academy
at West Point, New York.

Suzanne's father became one of the many U.S. soldiers fighting in Vietnam, a small divided country in Southeast Asia. Since 1964, the United States had poured massive amounts of military, political, and economic aid into the country to help South Vietnam maintain its independence from communist North Vietnam. By 1968, at the peak of U.S. military involvement, 500,000 American soldiers were serving in Vietnam. Although many Americans vehemently protested their country's participation in the war, officials continued drafting nearly 35,000 more men each month.

It was an anxious, troubling time for Suzanne and her family. Flickering television images on the nightly news reports brought the war's carnage into their living room. Although Jane Collins tried to shield her children, sometimes newscasts aired after the cartoons Suzanne watched. She heard the word Vietnam often, and the graphic images on the television screen terrified her. Suzanne understood her father was in Vietnam, a dangerous, threatening place where people died. Even at the age of six, she realized that war shaped her family's fate. As an adult, Suzanne would remember the frightening time she endured during the Vietnam War. "If your parent is deployed and you are that young, you spend the whole time wondering where they are and waiting for them to come home," Suzanne said. "As time passes and the absence is longer and longer, you become more and more concerned—but you don't really have the words to express your concern. There's only this continued absence."

Wounded servicemen arrive from Vietnam at Andrews Air Force Base in Maryland in 1968.

In 1975, by the time the last American troops left Vietnam, an estimated 58,226 American soldiers, 1 million Vietnamese soldiers, and 4 million Vietnamese citizens had been killed. Suzanne's father was one of the lucky ones who returned home. However, like numerous soldiers who served in Vietnam, he suffered nightmares for the rest of his life. At times, Suzanne awoke to the sound of her father crying out during his terrible dreams.

Michael Collins wanted his children to understand what he did for a living and what he had experienced. Suzanne's father schooled his four children in military history, just as he had taught cadets at West Point. He challenged them to question whether

the benefit of a battle outweighed its costs. "I believe he felt a great responsibility and urgency about
educating his children about war," Suzanne said.

> He would take us frequently to places like
> battlefields and war monuments. It would
> start back with whatever had precipitated
> the war and moved up through the battle-
> field you were standing in and through that
> and after that. It was a very comprehensive
> tour guide experience. So, throughout our
> lives, we basically heard about war.

Suzanne's father also taught his children about
politics and economics. He had grown up during

the Great Depression, an economic crisis following a devastating stock market crash in 1929. The Great Depression affected the rich and the poor; an estimated 15 million people suffered from unemployment. Suzanne's father told stories about the grim Depression years. His family, like many, had lived from meal to meal. Out of necessity, to put food on the table, he hunted and learned to pick edible plants. As an adult, Suzanne's father sometimes gathered wild mushrooms from the woods. Suzanne's mother worried they might be poisonous, or even deadly, and didn't let her children eat the mushrooms he brought home and cooked. However, Suzanne's father never got sick from eating them.

The Lion's Mound on the site of the Battle of Waterloo in Braine-l'Alleud, Belgium

When Suzanne wasn't learning about history from her father, she enjoyed gymnastics, reading, and playing in the woods. She dreamed of becoming an actress. Due to her father's career, Suzanne's family moved frequently. Sometimes Suzanne found making friends to be difficult because she often felt like a stranger. A self-described military brat, Suzanne was a quiet, but confident, girl with fine features and long reddish-blond hair.

The year Suzanne turned eleven, the Air Force moved the Collinses to Brussels, Belgium. Suzanne's father seized the opportunity to teach his children about the region's violent past. "And this was Europe, which is one gigantic battlefield," Suzanne said. Trips to castles turned into lessons about strongholds.

"My dad's holding me back from the tour to show me where they poured the boiling oil, where the arrow slits are. And then you're just like, wait a minute! This isn't what I had in mind . . . I should have known better."

Fortunately, her father had a gift for making history come alive.

In Europe, Suzanne was exposed to new customs and different languages. Belgium is a bilingual country; its citizens speak French and Flemish. Suzanne learned some French and a smattering of Flemish. Once, on a ferry crossing from Belgium to England, Suzanne clambered onto a tank aboard the ship to get a better view of the North Sea. The Flemish phrase she remembers best is the one a guard told her that day: *you cannot climb on the tank.*

From seventh to tenth grade, Suzanne attended an American school in Belgium. Her favorite teacher was Ms. Vance, who taught English, a subject Suzanne adored. On rainy days, Ms. Vance took any interested students aside and read aloud to them. Suzanne especially liked when Ms. Vance read stories by Edgar Allan Poe. She sat wide-eyed and riveted to *The Telltale Heart* and *The Mask of the Red Death*. Ms. Vance didn't think the students were too young to hear the suspenseful stories, a fact that made a big impression on Suzanne.

Living overseas, the Collins family watched little television. They had a house full of books, and Suzanne was an avid reader. "I think it's important for everyone to read," she said:

It exposes you to people and places and times and ideas that you might never encounter or encounter in such an intimate way. There's this one on one connection. No one's interpreting the material for you. It's this opportunity for your mind to meet the writer's mind. Grab it.

Suzanne especially enjoyed the novels *1984*, *Lord of the Flies*, *A Wrinkle in Time*, and *The Phantom Tollbooth*.

Suzanne inherited her mother's passion for fantasy and mythology. Jane Collins also loved fashion, a trait her youngest daughter didn't share. Suzanne devoured *D'Aulaires' Book of Greek Myths*, becoming especially fascinated by the story of Theseus and the Minotaur—a tale of ruthless punishment, bravery, and love. The myth is set in the aftermath of a war between the ancient cities of Athens and Crete. Although Athens initiated the war, Crete emerged victorious. Each year, as retribution, King Minos of Crete forces the Athenians to send seven boys and seven girls to Crete. There, they are thrown into a labyrinth, or maze, to be devoured by a monster called the Minotaur, a creature that was half-bull, half-man.

"Even when I was a child I was blown away by how evil that was," said Collins. "It was like Crete was sending this very clear message which was, if you mess with us, we will do something worse than kill you. We will kill your children."

In the myth, Theseus, the Athenian king's son, volunteers to take the place of one of the youths sent to Crete. King Minos's daughter, Ariadne, falls in love with Theseus and helps him to slay the Minotaur. Theseus's brave, selfless act stuck firmly in Suzanne's mind. One day, she would use the concept in her own book.

When the Collins family returned to the United States, Suzanne began attending the Alabama School of Fine Arts in Birmingham, Alabama. Located in the heart of the city's cultural district,

An 1843 sculpture by Antoine-Louis Barye of Theseus slaying the Minotaur

the school offers instruction to about three hundred students in seventh through twelfth grade. Education focuses on creative writing, dance, music, theater, and visual arts. Students also take core academic courses to earn their high school diplomas. To be accepted at the selective school, they write essays and undergo interviews and auditions. The Alabama School of Fine Arts offers one of the best theater programs in the southeastern United States.

The school's theater department especially interested Suzanne. As a Theater Arts major, she learned all phases of a production—from props to technical aspects to acting. Suzanne studied subjects such as mime, traditional dance styles, acting for the camera, and how to survive in the theater business. She also performed different types of plays, some for children, and others demonstrating a specific acting and design style.

In Birmingham, rich cultural opportunities surrounded Suzanne. Close at hand were art galleries, theaters, and concert halls where she could gaze at priceless works of art and attend operas, symphonies, and ballets. The Birmingham Children's Theater, one of the country's oldest and largest children's theaters, stood just footsteps away.

In the spring of 1980, Suzanne graduated from the Theater Arts program. After graduation, she made plans to leave the South behind and return to the Midwest. Suzanne had been accepted at Indiana University in Bloomington, Indiana, where she intended to pursue her longtime goal of acting.

From Acting
to Writing

In September 1980, Collins set foot on the campus of Indiana University. She found herself among a sea of students at a large university in rural Indiana, vastly different from her small urban high school. Located in Bloomington, an hour south of Indianapolis, the sprawling campus is dotted with green spaces and buildings constructed from local limestone. A small stream, the Jordan River, threads its way through the university's grounds.

The university's reputation in the arts had attracted Collins. Its alumni include award-winning musicians, dancers, actors, and writers, like Meg Cabot who penned *The Princess Diaries*, and Jeri Taylor, screenwriter of *Star Trek: The Next Generation*. Indiana University is home to the Lilly Library, one of the largest collections of rare books and manuscripts in the United States. Within its walls lie classic plays, such as the first printed collection of William Shakespeare's works and J. M. Barrie's *Peter Pan*. Collins planned to study theater and drama.

While attending Indiana University, Collins was involved in several theater productions. In *The Prime of Miss Jean Brodie*, she starred in the role of Jenny, a young, pretty student at a conservative girls' school. She also had a part in *Forest Game*, a thriller set deep in a national forest. The play told the tale of a forest ranger named Norman caught between the demands of a logging company and an environmental group. The play was set on the front porch of the forest ranger's cabin. Collins played the role of Becky, Norman's despairing wife. Charles Allen Pryor, Cap for short, starred as the ranger.

A senior like Collins, Cap was studying telecommunications. He enjoyed the challenge of acting in *Forest Game*, an original play that was rewritten several times. "We like the rewrites a lot," he said. "It's like Christmas when we get them."

Cap, the son of Charles and Dixie Pryor, loved films and filmmaking and appeared in a number of university productions. He starred as both Cain and Satan in *The Play of Adam*, a drama based on an eight hundred-year-old medieval play. Pryor also was cast as a lieutenant in *Arsenic and Old Lace*, a show staged at the historic Brown County Playhouse. A short drive from the university, located in the nineteenth century artists' colony of Nashville, the playhouse had been in operation since the 1930s.

Collins and Pryor found they shared many interests. Drawn together by their love of the theater, the two would one day marry each other. They both graduated from Indiana University in 1985. Collins earned her bachelor's degree, with honors, in telecommunications and theater and drama. Pryor received a degree in telecommunications.

After graduation, Collins held several jobs. She found work as a disc jockey at a country western music station and also performed data entry for a yearbook company. For a time, she took a job as a local news reporter for NPR, National Public Radio. Although Collins had long planned a career in acting, her focus was shifting. She wanted to do more than just speak the words on stage—she wanted to write them. When Collins tried her hand at writing a one-act play, she got hooked and realized she wanted to become a writer. As Collins changed career directions, she drew on the support she had received from her parents and teachers over the years.

"They always allowed me to believe that it was a possibility that I could be a writer as my profession," Collins said. "It wasn't just a thing that other people did, but that I could do it too, and they encouraged me to follow that dream."

At twenty-five years old, Collins decided to go back to school to study dramatic writing. She enrolled in New York University, where she planned to earn her master of fine arts (MFA), a graduate degree requiring her to spend an additional two or three years in school. She would attend the Tisch School of the Arts, one of the fifteen schools that make up New York University. Part of the university for more than forty-five years, the Tisch School of the Arts is one of the most distinguished writing programs in the country. The dramatic writing program, one of the smaller departments, has approximately forty graduate students.

Collins planned to concentrate on playwriting, screenwriting, and television writing. She would be able to develop her craft by working closely with some of the most accomplished novelists and poets of the time. All of the faculty members in the dramatic writing program are working professionals in their fields—from experimental theater and Broadway to independent films and major Hollywood movies. In television, they represent everything from major television networks to HBO. In order to graduate, Collins would need to complete a full-scale work for theater, television, or film.

Collins found herself in a different world— the bustling, noisy streets of New York City. NYU's campus stretches from Wall Street to Midtown Manhattan, with Washington Square Park resting at its heart. To enter the park's quiet haven, visitors walk under a large white marble arch. Fringed with flowerbeds and trees, the park features a 310-year-old tree named Hangman's Elm, the oldest known tree in New York City.

Tisch School of the Arts is located in the middle of Greenwich Village. Known since the late 1800s as an artists' haven, Greenwich Village was once a rural hamlet just north of the settlement on Manhattan Island. Unlike the high-rise landscape of downtown Manhattan,

Washington Square Park in New York City

the colorful village features nineteenth century row houses and mid-rise apartments. Its narrow streets curve at odd angles. Greenwich Village has long been a hot spot for aspiring playwrights. New York City's oldest off-Broadway theater, Cherry Lane Theater, was established there in 1924, and other theaters had quickly followed suit. Some of the world's greatest theaters, museums, art galleries, music halls, and bookstores stood just a few blocks away from Collins's new home.

While Collins studied at NYU, Cap Pryor attended graduate school at Penn State University, in rural central Pennsylvania. Like Collins, he was earning his MFA. Soon each graduated, and they began their lives together in New York City: Collins as a writer and Pryor as an actor.

Freshly armed with her degree in dramatic writing, Collins was ready to begin a career in television writing. Her talent and strong background in the arts quickly earned her a job. For a little more than a year, she worked in development for a film producer before scoring a television writing job in 1991.

Collins first found television work on the live action show *Hi Honey, I'm Home!* The program followed the Nielsons, an American sitcom family from the 1950s living in 1990s suburbia. Through the supposed Sitcom Relocation Program, the Nielsons had been transported to the real world after the cancellation of their show. *Hi Honey, I'm Home!* featured guest appearances from actors who had starred in classic television shows. The program was on the air for a year, thirteen episodes, before being canceled.

Next, Collins found work writing for the children's television series *Clarissa Explains it All*. Based on the life of a character named Clarissa Darling, the show ran on Nickelodeon for five seasons. Melissa Joan Hart, the actress who played Clarissa, won a Young Artist Award. *Clarissa Explains it All* marked the start of Collins's longtime career in children's television programming.

Collins realized her writing style fit young audiences well, in spite of her future renown writing darker stories for older children. In television, writers create sixty-five episodes, after which the show can be syndicated, or sold to multiple television stations. With numerous episodes to write, Collins learned how to develop story characters that children could relate to—whether the characters were dogs, sea creatures, or other kids.

Collins also found she had a knack for keeping audiences interested. She understood how to time a script so characters teetered on the verge of peril or a revelation just before a commercial break. The suspense kept her viewers tuned into the program. This skill would one day translate to her work as an author, spurring her readers to keep turning pages as they devoured her books.

"I find there isn't a great deal of difference technically in how you approach a story, no matter what age it's for," Collins said, adding:

> I started out as a playwright for adult audiences. When television work came along, it was primarily for children. But whatever age you're writing for, the same rules of plot, character, and theme apply. You just set up a world and try to remain true to it. If it's filled with cuddly animated animals, chances are no one's going to die. If it's filled with giant flesh-and-blood rats with a grudge, there's going to be violence.

Collins's early years as a writer were busy and eventful. In 1994, she and Pryor had their first child, a son they named Charlie. Shortly after, Collins started writing for the animated show *Little Bear*. Based on a children's book by Maurice Sendak, *Little Bear* followed the adventures of a bear cub discovering the world. The popular show ran for five seasons on Nick Jr. and was nominated for an Emmy Award.

Emmy Awards, or Emmys, honor excellence in television programming. They are the television equivalent to the Academy Awards for movies and the Grammy Awards for music. The Academy of Television Arts and Sciences, and other television organizations, award Emmys in different categories, such as prime time and daytime shows, sports programs, news, and documentaries. First awarded in 1949 in a small ceremony honoring local programming in Los Angeles, today the awards are a national event. The golden Emmy statue depicts a winged woman holding an atom. The wings represent the muse of art; the atom represents the electron of science. Originally, the Academy planned to call the statue Ike, after president Dwight D. Eisenhower's nickname. They changed their minds and named it Immy, an abbreviation for image orthicon, part of a television camera. They later feminized the name to Emmy. Winning an Emmy Award is one of the highest honors a television program or television actor can achieve.

Collins's husband was also finding success in his field. He performed internationally and scored principal roles on network and cable television shows.

An Emmy statue

Pryor also kept busy as a founding member of Synchronicity Theater Group, or STG. Pryor directed the company in several plays and starred in the group's productions *Enemy of the People* and *The Trial*. STG was located in SoHo, a trendy neighborhood in Lower Manhattan. The name SoHo refers to the area <u>So</u>uth of <u>Ho</u>uston Street. Known for its artists' lofts and galleries, SoHo also features the largest collection of cast iron architecture in the world. More than two hundred cast iron buildings, with decorative facades, graceful curved window frames, and sleek columns, line the streets.

In 1996, Collins started working on *The Mystery Files of Shelby Woo*, a show about a young girl who lives with her grandfather and solves crimes in her spare time. Collins wrote several episodes and served as the executive story editor for a number of others. The show ran from 1996 to 1999 and was nominated for a Writers Guild of America award. The yearly award, presented by the Writers Guild, recognizes outstanding achievements in film, television, and radio.

Next, Collins was hired as the head writer for the show *Generation O!* She wrote most of the program's thirteen episodes, telling the story of Molly O, an eight-year-old rock star in the band Generation O. Each episode featured a song and a music video related to the story. When *Generation O!* went off the air in 2001, Collins quickly found a job on the animated Nick Jr. show *Oswald*. She wrote episodes about a blue octopus named Oswald and his friends: a dog, a penguin, and a duck, named Weenie, Henry, and Daisy. Around this time, Collins and her husband had their second child, a daughter they named Isabel.

In 2003, Collins received a nomination from the Writers Guild of America for her work on *Santa, Baby!*, an animated Christmas special she co-wrote with Peter Bakalian. Rankin/Bass, a production company known for their seasonal television specials like *Frosty the Snowman* and *Rudolph's Shiny New Year*, produced the show. Based on a Christmas song, the special told the story of Noel, a frustrated songwriter trying to write a hit song. The story featured primarily African American characters and the voices of Gregory Hines, Eartha Kitt, and Vanessa Williams.

Soon after, Collins became the head writer for *Clifford's Puppy Days* and began dreaming up stories involving an oversized, goofy red dog. A spin off of the original series *Clifford the Big Red Dog*, the animated show featured Clifford as a puppy, the runt of the litter, and his owner, Emily. It aired from 2003 to 2004 on PBS Kids.

Clifford the Big Red Dog in a parade in Chile

Collins's career and growing family kept her busy. With two children, she and her husband realized their apartment was bursting at the seams. In need of more space, they decided to move their family to Sandy Hook, Connecticut, a small town about two hours from New York City. Unlike the concrete jungle of the city, the village of Sandy Hook is dotted with antique colonial homes and surrounded by parks, forests, and the Housatonic and Pootatuck rivers. Collins and her family soon settled in, adopting the two feral, or wild, kittens living in their backyard, and naming them Zorro and Zable.

Sandy Hook, Connecticut

The move to Connecticut wasn't the only change Collins hoped to make. While working on *Generation O!* she had become good friends with James Proimos, the show's creator. Proimos had worked on other television shows and screenplays, along with illustrating and writing several children's books, such as *The Loudness of Sam* and *Patricia von Pleasant Squirrel.* Proimos suggested Collins give writing books a try. "She seemed like a book writer to me; it was sort of her personality," Proimos said:

> She also had the style and the mind of a novelist. I was telling her that you can't do TV forever; it's a young person's business. With books, at the very worst, you start out slow, but you can do them for the rest of your life.

Collins decided to listen to her friend. She would be leaving behind the world of eleven-minute animated television episodes about gigantic red dogs and curious bear cubs. Just as she had successfully evolved from actress to television writer, she now planned to make the leap to author.

Ǝ
Creating the Underland

As Collins settled into her new home, she began working on her first book. Collins's background in scriptwriting served her well. Writing a book had many of the same demands as writing a television script or play. First, Collins would consider the arc of the story, establishing its skeleton, or outline, in her mind. Next, she would concentrate on developing a strong plot and characters that were relatable to her audience. As with television commercial breaks, Collins wanted to end her chapters on cliffhangers to keep readers interested in the story. She planned for the book to be divided into three sections, each with nine chapters. It was a comfortable structure for her, resembling the three-act plays she once wrote. Although Collins had enjoyed collaborating with others over television scripts, she loved that a book allowed her to conceive an idea and carry it through by herself.

Collins consulted her fellow author friends James Proimos and Christopher Santos. Collins and Santos shared a similar background. Santos held an MFA in dramatic writing from New York University and had worked in New York City as a script reader and story editor. He had also written the novels *Wanderlust* and *The Loves of a D-Girl*. Both Santos and Proimos offered encouragement to Collins.

Proimos suggested Collins contact his literary agent, Rosemary Stimola, the owner of Stimola Literary Studio. Her company represents authors who write fiction and nonfiction for children and young adults. With a PhD in linguistics, Stimola formerly taught language and literature at the City University of New York. Specializing in children's literature, she loved bringing kids and books together. She also owned A Child's Story, an independent bookstore in New Jersey. Stimola requested that Collins send in a sample chapter of her manuscript.

As Collins mulled over ideas, she remembered the mythology she loved reading as a child. According to Collins, her favorites had been the stories of "very dramatic and terrible things like someone cooking their kids up and feeding them to a god, or a woman murdering her children in revenge for her husband's unfaithfulness." Collins wanted her book to have the same flavor.

Collins began to think about the children's book *Alice in Wonderland* and how foreign its country backdrop must seem to children like her own who lived in urban settings. Alice had tumbled down a rabbit hole into a different world. Collins imagined her main character plunging down a New York City manhole. Instead of finding a tea party, like Alice, he would find the Underland, a subterranean world with the gritty feel of New York City, populated by the Underlanders, an unusual society of humans. The Underlanders shared their world with giant talking spiders, bats, rats, mice, and cockroaches—animals they referred to as spinners, fliers, gnawers, nibblers, and crawlers.

Said Collins:

> I liked the fact that this world was teeming under New York City and nobody was aware of it. That you could be going along preoccupied with your own problems and then whoosh! You take a wrong turn in your laundry room and suddenly a giant cockroach is right in your face. No magic, no space or time travel, there's just a ticket to another world behind your clothes dryer.

New York City's subway

In Collins's tale, Gregor, an eleven-year-old boy, lives in a cramped New York City apartment building with his mother, grandmother, and two younger sisters. His father had mysteriously disappeared months earlier. One hot summer day, while Gregor is washing clothes in the basement laundry room, his sister Margaret, nicknamed Boots, falls through a grate leading to the Underland. Gregor follows her and realizes his father could have disappeared in the same manner. While in the Underland, Gregor learns his father might be a prisoner of war, held hostage by rats. In order to rescue him, Gregor forms alliances with different characters and ventures into enemy territory, undertaking a journey that challenges him to survive physically and spiritually. The Underlanders come to believe Gregor is a warrior spoken of in age-old prophecies.

Collins recalled her childhood lessons about war and violence. Her father had discussed serious, tough topics with his children, despite their ages. Like him, Collins believed children could handle subjects far more difficult than many people assumed. Whatever type of story Collins told—whether for preschoolers or young adults—she wanted the leading character to be the age of the readers. She didn't want to write a war story for children and place the kids on the sidelines of the action. Collins decided the level of violence would be appropriate if she targeted the book towards middle grade readers. Setting her story in a fantasy world gave Collins the freedom to explore topics that might bother children in the present. The Underland resembles the real world in many ways, but, at the same time, remains a fantasy.

Collins didn't only rely on her childhood memories. She began reading stacks of books about bats, spiders, cockroaches, and rodents. During her research, she realized the ways in which other creatures are similar to humans and that all species share the same desire to survive. Collins especially enjoyed learning about bats. "I love bats," she said, "except these really loud ones that get in my attic in the summer and hold some kind of party all night long." Collins's husband gave her a large black wooden bat that reminded her of the character Ares, a brave bat in the Underland. She hung the bat in her kitchen and attached a rubber cockroach and stuffed spider to its back, recreating a scene from the book. The bat became one of her favorite presents.

Collins also researched the military aspects of her book. She spent hours on the phone with her father, plotting realistic combat strategies. In the Underland, two of the species, bats and humans, depend on each other in the battle against the rats. To Collins, the alliance made military sense because the bats are aerial fighters.

Collins found writing about Gregor to be easy. She had clear memories of being eleven years old, and many of her friends had been boys. In some ways, Collins shaped Gregor's character after herself. She remembered the anxiety she had sensed as a child when her father was fighting in the Vietnam War. Like her, Gregor's worries revolved around a missing parent. "I think I'm like Gregor because we both want to do the right thing but sometimes have trouble figuring out what it is," she said. "Also, neither of us likes to ride roller coasters and we've both changed a lot of diapers. But Gregor is much braver than I am . . . if I even see a regular sized rat in New York City I immediately cross the street."

Collins began to establish a writing routine, one she would continue throughout her career. Each morning, as soon as she awoke, she poured herself a bowl of cereal and sat down to write. Collins enjoyed the freedom of working at home in her pajamas if she wanted. She sometimes listened to music as she wrote, but preferred classical music, especially Mozart, because songs with lyrics interfered with her thought process. The more distractions Collins faced before she began writing, the harder it was for her to focus on the story. She usually worked until early afternoon, stopping after three to five hours of writing. Some days she just sat and stared at the wall, shaping the characters and plot in her mind. "The rest of the time, I walk around with the story slipping in and out of my thoughts," Collins said.

Developing the dialogue and action sequences came easily to Collins, because it was like giving stage directions. She found the descriptive passages of the book more difficult to write. Early in the book, Gregor walks through a curtain of moths and sees the underground city of Regalia. It took Collins a long time to write just the few paragraphs describing the city.

In a book, it's all up to you. I've finally accepted that no designer is going to step in and take care of the descriptive passages for me, so I've got to write them. But here's the great thing about writing books as opposed to screenwriting: there are no budget concerns. No one is ever going to tell you that they can't afford to build the set or to travel to a location or to do a special effect, and you're not going to write a scene that in your mind you set on the African veldt and there are herds of animals going by, and then, ultimately, you end up with one giraffe and one lion.

Within six months Collins had written her first draft, revising the story numerous times. She was no stranger to editing, having reworked one of her screenplays fourteen times before declaring it done. After a few months of polishing the story, she sent a chapter to Stimola. The literary agent quickly realized Collins knew how to tell a good story and hold the reader's attention. Stimola said:

Quite honestly, I knew from the very first paragraph I had a very gifted writer. It happens like that sometimes. Not often, but when it does, it's a thing of beauty. From the very first paragraph she established a character I cared about. She established a story and a mood that touched my heart.

Stimola submitted the manuscript to Scholastic, one of the world's largest publishers and distributors of children's books. Scholastic reaches more than 150 countries and has works in forty-five languages, publishing famous series like Goosebumps, The Magic School Bus, and Harry Potter. Before long, Scholastic accepted Collins's book. Scholastic editor Kate Egan, who had worked in publishing since the 1990s, began revising Collins's manuscript. Like Stimola, she couldn't put the book down.

Scholastic released *Gregor the Overlander* in 2003. At forty-one years old, Collins became a published author. She dedicated her first book to her parents. Sadly, Michael Collins never saw his daughter's success. He passed away shortly before *Gregor the Overlander* hit the bookshelves.

Soon Collins's book appeared on best seller lists, a rare accomplishment for a new novelist. From the onset, Collins envisioned *Gregor the Overlander* as the first book in a five-part series called The Underland Chronicles. Scholastic agreed to publish the rest of the series, and Collins began penning the next books about Gregor. Each year, for the following four years, Scholastic published another sequel in The Underland Chronicles. In 2004, *Gregor and the Prophecy of Bane* hit the shelves. In the book, Gregor returns to the Underland to rescue Boots after she is kidnapped by cockroaches. Next came *Gregor and the Curse of the Warmbloods,* in which Gregor helps the Underlanders find a cure for a plague that sickens his friends and family members.

Scholastic published other famous series such as Harry Potter.

While The Underland Chronicles was developing a loyal following, Collins wrote *When Charlie McButton Lost Power*, a book for younger readers. Her picture book tells about Charlie McButton, whose technological empire comes crashing down when a thunderstorm knocks out the electricity in his house. Charlie needs batteries to keep playing his games, but the only ones available are in his sister's favorite talking doll. The storm forces Charlie to snap out of his computer craze and have fun, without batteries. For illustrations, Collins teamed up with Mike Lester, an artist, animator, and writer. Lester's children's book *A is for Salad* had appeared on the *New York Times* Top 10 list in 2000.

Although Collins's picture book met with success, it was her books about Gregor and the Underland that captured readers' hearts. Hungry for more, people snapped up the next books in the series. They avidly read *Gregor and the Marks of Secret*, published in 2006, in which Gregor solves a mystery involving the mice population in the Underland. In the last installment, *Gregor and the Code of Claw*, Gregor returns to the Underland a final time to face a dangerous white rat he must destroy. Released in 2007, the series finale became a *New York Times* best seller.

Now a successful children's author, Collins realized she had found one of the loves of her life. "Somewhere along the way I realized I loved writing for kids," Collins said. "They're such an interesting audience because they're still making up their minds about things, about who they are, what they believe, what they think is right. They're also an extremely honest audience about what they like."

Despite Collins's early success, little did she know that her next books would take the world by storm.

4

The Hunger Games

Collins's next inspiration for a book struck one night while watching television. Lying in bed, channel surfing, she flipped back and forth between a reality television show and news coverage of the war in Iraq. On one channel, she watched young people competing for money. On the other, war footage showed children fighting for their actual survival. The newscast pulled Collins back to the time when she was a frightened young girl watching coverage of the Vietnam War and worrying about her father. Collins was tired and the images between the two shows blurred. They fused in her mind in a way that unsettled her. She wondered if viewers were becoming desensitized to the violence they saw on television and whether they could tell what was real and what was just a game.

An idea for a new book began to take shape in Collins's head. She would again draw from the myths she had loved as a child. "I was attracted to the myths because the people and the gods experience such a wide range of human emotions in this magical world," Collins said:

Really terrible things happen. A king cooks up his son into a stew. A sorceress turns every guy who lands on her island into a pig. There are great loves and great acts of courage. The world is a very unstable place, but the characters get along as best they can, and sometimes they manage remarkable things.

Collins focused on her favorite myth, Theseus and the Minotaur, which she first read at eight years old. She remembered how King Minos of Crete demanded the people of Athens send fourteen of their children to Crete each year to be thrown into the labyrinth with the deadly Minotaur. She thought about Theseus, the prince of Athens, who volunteered to go to Crete and then defeated the Minotaur.

Collins also recalled what she knew about ancient Roman gladiators. Ancient gladiators were armed combatants who battled other gladiators, condemned criminals, and animals. The Roman government had forced them to fight, sometimes to the death, as both punishment and entertainment.

During long Roman festivals, crowds had filled amphitheaters to watch an array of violent spectacles. They witnessed criminals sentenced to fight wild beasts without using weapons or armor, public executions featuring a variety of grisly torture, and staged animal hunts with exotic creatures, reminding Romans of the vast lands their empire had conquered. The gladiatorial games, one of the most popular forms of entertainment, typically occurred later in the day.

The majority of the Roman gladiators were slaves, condemned criminals, or prisoners of war. Others were volunteers and professionals who sought fame and monetary donations from the crowd. Although typically men, at times, female gladiators appeared in the arena. Criminals, who had less training than professional gladiators, were expected to die within a year. If they survived in the ring for three years, they could earn their release, receiving a wooden sword, or *rudis*, symbolizing their freedom.

Collins began to outline a novel combining a modern version of the Roman gladiatorial games, the myth of Theseus, and reality television. Many aspects of her story grew from classical roots. Collins planned to write about an annual televised event, called the Hunger Games, in which twelve boys and twelve girls fight to the death on live television. Resembling ancient gladiators, the twenty-four children, called tributes, have no choice but to participate in the games. The government forces them to battle each other and to contend with vicious animals in an arena in front of an audience.

Collins set her story in Panem, a futuristic world amid the ruins of North America. The name Panem came from the Roman phrase *Panem et Circenses* meaning "Bread and Circuses." It refers to the concept of citizens being too preoccupied with food and entertainment to take an active role in government and decision making. Panem, a country reduced by disasters and war, is comprised of twelve poverty-stricken districts that encircle a single decadent, glittering capitol. The government keeps the

An unofficial map of the fictional nation of Panem and its districts

SUZANNE COLLINS'S

PANEM

created by
aimmyarrowshigh.livejournal.com
& badguys.livejournal.com

citizens in the districts hungry and poor, as punishment for waging a war against the Capitol seventy-five years earlier.

Panem's leader, like King Minos, requires every district to send one boy and one girl, between the ages of twelve and eighteen, to fight in the annual Hunger Games. During ceremonies called reapings, each district draws two names to select their tributes. Panem's citizens are required to watch the televised Hunger Games, bearing witness as their children slay each other on live television. The winner of the games is the one left standing.

Collins named her main character Katniss, after an edible plant she read about in a wilderness survival book. Katniss's last name, Everdeen, came from a character in *Far From the Madding Crowd*, a novel by Thomas Hardy. Like Bathsheba Everdeen, Katniss struggles to know her own heart. One of Panem's impoverished citizens, Katniss was eleven years old when her father died in a coal mining accident. She became her family's sole provider, hunting illegally in the nearby woods to keep her mother and sister alive. When Katniss's little sister Prim is chosen during the reaping, Katniss, like Theseus, volunteers to go in her place. During the Hunger Games, Katniss develops into a tough-as-nails, modern-day gladiator, despite being torn between her feelings for Peeta, her fellow tribute, and Gale, a hunting friend. Collins's working title for the book was *The Tribute of District Twelve*; soon it simply became *The Hunger Games*.

The katniss plant is native to South, Central, and North America and goes by many names, such as arrowhead, duck potato, and wapato.

When developing Katniss's character, Collins drew from one of her favorite movies—*Spartacus*. Based on a true story, Spartacus was a Roman slave who escaped from the gladiator ring and inspired slaves to rise up in rebellion against the Roman Empire. Like Spartacus, Katniss would transform herself from slave to gladiator to rebel.

Bits and pieces of Collins's life shaped other aspects of Katniss's personality. Collins's book characters, first Gregor and now Katniss, played out the childhood anxiety Collins had faced due to an absent parent. Like Collins's father, who suffered nightmares after his tour of duty in Vietnam, Katniss, and other characters who participate in the Hunger Games, are haunted by memories of violence.

Collins's experiences in television also inspired elements of the book. When Katniss arrives in the Capitol before the Hunger Games, she is made over by a crew of makeup artists and fashion designers. The notion of a team creating personas for the tributes and adapting a world to create a television show was loosely based on Collins's work in television. "In a way, it's very easy for me to imagine the world of the Gamemakers, because in a much gentler way I was one myself," said Collins.

With the idea firmly planted in her head, Collins went to work. She read piles of outdoor survival books because her main character needed to know how to stay alive in the woods. Collins also recalled some sword training she had taken. Settled in a La-Z-Boy chair, she typed away on her laptop. Parts of the book would be difficult for her to write, especially the violent war scenes between children.

"When you're going to write a story like *The Hunger Games*, you have to accept from the beginning that you're going to kill characters," Collins said. "It's a horrible thing to do, and it's a horrible thing to write, particularly when you have to take out a character that is vulnerable or young or someone you've grown to love when you were writing them."

Collins remembered how her father taught his children about war and violence. She considered the manner in which she told her own children about these subjects, carefully treading the line between details they needed to know and gratuitous violence. Because of the topic, children-on-children violence, Collins wrote her book for young adults, targeting a slightly older audience than she had for The Underland Chronicles.

At times when working on *The Hunger Games*, Collins took breaks from the dark world of Panem by writing an episode of *Wow! Wow! Wubbzy!*, an animated children's television show for which she sometimes wrote. *Wow! Wow! Wubbzy!* followed the adventures of a happy yellow cat, named Wubbzy, who explored the world with his friends. Diving into the imaginary town of Wuzzleburg, the setting for the preschool show, provided a mental break for Collins. "It's an enormous relief to spend some hours in Wuzzleburg, writing an eleven-minute episode, where I know things are going to work out just fine and all the characters will be alive at the end of the program."

Despite the difficult subject, within ten months Collins had shaped the first draft of what would become her best-known novel. She typed up a three-and-a-half page proposal to send to Scholastic, the company that published The Underland Chronicles. Collins wrote, "Although set in the future, *The Hunger Games* explores disturbing issues of modern warfare such as who fights our wars, how they are orchestrated, and the ever-increasing opportunities to observe them being played out."

The proposal got an immediate reaction from the editors at Scholastic. David Levithan, executive editorial director at Scholastic, said:

> I remember that the manuscript came in on a Friday, and I read it over the weekend. Two other people read it—Kate Egan, Suzanne's longtime editor, and Jennifer Rees, an editor who was also working on the books. On Monday morning, we were dying to talk to each other—it was simply one of the most astonishing things we'd ever read. Our editorial conversation pretty much consisted of one word: *Wow.*

Scholastic snapped up *The Hunger Games*, offering Collins a six-figure deal. Although Egan had left Scholastic to become a freelance editor, part of Collins's deal with Scholastic was that Egan stay on as her editor. After working closely on The Underland Chronicles, the two trusted each other and worked well together. Egan realized this would be the most important book she had ever edited.

The suspenseful book with the twisting plot quickly became an in-house favorite at Scholastic. Blown away by the story, people in Scholastic's sales, marketing, and publicity departments busily created a buzz storm about Collins's book. As a promotional tool before publication of *The Hunger Games*, Scholastic sent out advance reading copies to booksellers and librarians, many of whom devoured the book in one sitting. Scholastic planned a first printing of 50,000 copies, then doubled it, and doubled it again as word spread. Collins's agent began selling foreign rights to publishers around the world, and Collins embarked on a book tour across the United States to promote *The Hunger Games*.

Illustrator Tim O'Brien, who designed the cover of the book, focused on the mockingjay, a fictional bird in the story. To spy on the rebels during the war years, the Capitol had genetically engineered the jabberjay, a small black bird that recorded everything it heard. Instead of dying out after the Capitol's plan failed, jabberjays bred with female mockingbirds to create a new species, the mockingjay. Katniss wears a mockingjay pin on her clothes as a good luck charm during the games. For many in Panem, the mockingjay becomes a symbol of the rebellion brewing in the districts. O'Brien featured the golden mockingjay pin on the book's black cover.

In October 2008, *The Hunger Games* hit the shelves and became an instant phenomenon. Within two months, *The Hunger Games* had topped several best seller lists, including the *New York Times* list, where it stayed for more than three consecutive years. The book collected numerous awards, and several magazines and newspapers named it the Best Book of 2008.

 The Hunger Games combines violence, love, sorrow, and politics, entrancing both young and older adult readers. "It's one of those properties that crosses all boundaries," said Levithan. "Some readers

top right: Collins's mockingjay necklace. The pendant is a depiction of the pin that Katniss wore during the Hunger Games.
bottom left: Suzanne Collins poses in 2008 with her book.

will latch onto the horrific scenarios, others will latch onto the dystopian war story, the love story, the evolution of the characters, the sci-fi aspects . . . No two people will have the same experience with the [story], much like Harry Potter."

Passed on from reader to reader, praise for *The Hunger Games* spread like wildfire. Fan Web sites popped up across the Internet. Spurred by their students' enthusiasm, teachers began to use the book in their classrooms. A seventh-grade teacher in New Jersey persuaded her school to buy sixty copies, after she saw students fighting over her personal copy. Students clamored for Collins to come to their schools. When she visited a middle school in Plainfield, Illinois, students created a mock tribute parade in the gym. After Collins's presentation, they lowered a silver parachute by pulley from the ceiling. It contained a mockingjay necklace that Collins still wears today.

Despite the excitement over *The Hunger Games*, Collins continued to focus on her writing. She had known from the beginning The Hunger Games was a three-book series. Collins said:

> Once I'd thought through to the end of the book, I realized that there was no way that the story was concluded. Katniss does something that would never go unpunished in her world. There would definitely be repercussions. And so the question of whether or not to continue with the series was answered for me.

Collins tentatively named her second book *The Quarter Quell*, although its title eventually became *Catching Fire*. In the continuation of Katniss's story, the Capitol forces her to fight in the following year's Hunger Games by requiring districts to send tributes who won past games. Katniss stands at the heart of the rebellion rising against the Capitol.

In September 2009, *Catching Fire* debuted at number one on the *New York Times*, *Publishers Weekly*, *Wall Street Journal*, and *USA Today* best seller lists. Fans snapped up copies of *Catching Fire* and in just fourteen months more than 1.5 million copies of the first two books in the series were in print in North America alone. Respected newspapers and magazines named it the Best Book

Stephenie Meyer

of 2009 and the Best Children's Book of 2009. Other authors praised the book too. "*Catching Fire* not only lived up to my high expectations, it surpassed them," said Stephenie Meyer, of the Twilight series. "It's just as exciting as *The Hunger Games*, but even more gut wrenching, because you already know these characters, you've already suffered with them."

Little had Collins known that when she created the fictional world of Panem, her own world would change. After rocketing to fame, life for the forty-nine-year-old author was no longer the same. As a television writer, Collins had remained relatively anonymous, often sharing credit with other writers. Now a celebrity, she stood alone in the spotlight. The overwhelming reaction surprised Collins, and the attention made her uncomfortable. Collins's two children enjoyed teasing their mother about her newfound fame.

In April of 2010, Collins was named to the *Time 100* list. Each year, *Time* magazine releases an issue noting the artists, leaders, heroes, and thinkers who most affected the world that year. Collins shared the list with singer Lady Gaga, former president Bill Clinton, and Apple co-founder Steve Jobs. In December, *Entertainment Weekly* labeled Collins one of the Entertainers of the Year, and *Fast Company*, a magazine dedicated to recognizing cutting edge entrepreneurs, named her to their 100 Most Creative People in Business list.

Fans clamored to learn more about Collins and began calling her at home. Although none of the fans were threatening, Collins changed her number to protect her family's privacy. Becoming famously media shy, she refused most interview requests. Balancing author visits and book promotions with writing became challenging. Wanting to finish telling Katniss's story, Collins tried to block out the attention as best she could. "You sort of do have to work to construct walls of silence," she said.

I can't go online. I can't listen to a lot of Internet discussion about it. It's not helpful to my writing process." Collins didn't want her readers' opinions to change the story she planned to tell.

Despite having two books in the series under her belt, Collins still found the violent aspects difficult to write. She enjoyed the parts in which Katniss reflected on the happier moments in her life. In the final book, titled *Mockingjay*, Katniss becomes the symbol of a full-scale rebellion against the Capitol. She fights to stay alive and to keep her friends and family safe. When Collins gave the manuscript to her agent, Stimola read avidly until the last chapter, in which a firebombing kills innocent civilians and characters. Reacting as a reader, emotionally attached to the story, she called Collins. "No!" Stimola wailed. "Don't do it." Collins told her, "Oh, but it has to be. This is not a fairy tale; it's a war, and in war, there are tragic losses that must be mourned."

Fans around the world waited anxiously for the final book in the series. Merchandise based on The Hunger Games flooded stores and the Internet. Collins wanted the story to be a surprise until it hit the bookshelves, and Scholastic kept the book under tight wraps, not even printing advance reading copies. "I've never worked on a project that was so top secret," said Levithan. "I actually had to wipe the file from my laptop when I was done with it, for fear that I'd be the guy who leaves his laptop in a taxi and ends up ruining it for everyone."

Josie, sixteen, reads *The Hunger Games*
in Grand Rapids, Michigan.

Scholastic's Web site featured an online countdown clock, contests, and activity kits for booksellers. Similar to the release of books in the Harry Potter series, bookstores scheduled midnight parties for the debut of *Mockingjay*. For her first-ever midnight release party, Collins planned to go to Books of Wonder, a bookstore in New York City. Despite the excitement, she urged readers not to stay home from school the next day to read her book. "At the risk of sounding ungrateful, please go to school," she said. "So many kids in the world never get a chance to. That being said, if you wanted to stay up late reading, I wouldn't be the one taking the flashlight away from you."

Scholastic released *Mockingjay* on August 24, 2010, with 1.2 million copies in its first printing. It sold 450,000 copies in the United States in its first week and topped all national best seller lists. Scholastic quickly went back to press to print another 800,000 books. Within two months, there were 2 million copies in print in the United States. Soon, Collins embarked on a twelve-city book tour, visiting bookstores from Boston to Seattle. She delighted her readers everywhere she went. Scholastic's Ellie Berger said, "After months of anticipation, sales for *Mockingjay* have exceeded all expectations, as has the outpouring from countless teen and adult fans of the trilogy who have been blogging, tweeting and coming out to meet Suzanne Collins on the first leg of her North American tour."

To choose a stop along Collins's tour, Scholastic held a bookstore display contest. Powell's Books in Portland, Oregon, won a visit by constructing a seventeen-foot-long cornucopia, representing a scene from the books. "A visit from The Hunger Games series author, Suzanne Collins, is better than birthdays and snow days!" said Suzy Wilson from the store's children's team.

Collins's trilogy had joined the ranks of famed young adult fantasy series like Harry Potter and Twilight. Although there would be no more books in The Hunger Games series, fans wanted more. Soon they would get their wish. Collins's plans for *The Hunger Games* weren't over yet.

The Big Screen

The stir over The Hunger Games trilogy captured the attention of people in Hollywood. Production companies were approaching Collins about the opportunity to make a movie version of *The Hunger Games*. Although she had been busy writing and promoting the books, eventually, she talked to several producers over the phone. Collins wanted to choose the one who would best adapt *The Hunger Games* to the big screen.

One of the producers Collins spoke to was Nina Jacobson of Color Force Productions. Jacobson produced the movies *The Chronicles of Narnia* and *Pirates of the Caribbean*. Shortly after *The Hunger Games* was published, one of Jacobson's employees recommended she read the book. "I just picked it up, couldn't put it down, and spent a lot of the time that I was reading it thinking, How can you make a movie that has violence between young people?" Jacobson said. "And yet, as I saw the way that Suzanne had walked that line, by staying inside Katniss's character and managing to comment on the violence without ever exploiting it, I became more convinced there was a way that a movie could do the same."

She added, "I became pretty much obsessed with the book and then couldn't bear the thought that anybody else would produce the film." Liking how Jacobson connected to the story and carefully considered its violent aspects, Collins chose her to produce the movie version of *The Hunger Games*.

Next, Collins and Jacobson set about finding a movie studio. Many vied for the job. After meeting with several, they picked Lionsgate, a movie and television entertainment company. Lionsgate produces shows on more than ten networks. In 2010, with Academy Award-winning films like *Precious*, Lionsgate's film business generated more than $.5 billion in box offices in North America. "Lionsgate is known for fearlessness—we have never shied away from bold projects that stir up conversation," said Joe Drake, president of Lionsgate's motion picture group. "But we don't make projects simply because they're edgy . . . we are always looking for quality stories that are character driven. So it wasn't anything controversial that drew us to *The Hunger Games*—it was the irresistible character of Katniss."

A long line of directors hoped to work on the film. One of them was Gary Ross, who directed *Seabiscuit*, a movie nominated for seven Academy Awards, including Best Picture. Ross read *The Hunger Games* after hearing his fifteen-year-old twins rave about the books. "I mentioned *The Hunger Games* to my kids, and they exploded, went on and on, and I had to actually stop them from telling me the entire story," Ross said. "So I went upstairs, started reading around ten o'clock at night, and finished around one-thirty in the morning. I literally put the book down and said, 'I have to make this movie. I just have to.'" Ross flew to England to meet with Jacobson, who was on a movie set in London. He put together a powerful documentary featuring teenagers talking about what *The Hunger Games* meant to them. Ross's presentation blew people at Lionsgate away, and he quickly clinched the role of director.

Gary Ross at the world premiere of *The Hunger Games* on March 12, 2012, in Los Angeles

Jacobson said:

> I felt very protective of the book. There was
> a version of the movie that could be made
> that would in fact be guilty of all of the sins of
> the Capitol and portray this violence among
> youth irresponsibly. If you put the visual wow
> as your priority over the character of Katniss,
> you risk making junk food out of something
> which is anything but. And Gary had a real
> feel for the balancing act between the epic ad-
> venture and the intimate love story.

With a producer, movie studio, and director in place, Collins began the challenging job of writing the screenplay. She needed to condense the 384-page book into a two-hour movie. She also had to tell the story in third-person perspective, unlike the book's first-person perspective, but still show Katniss's inner world. Collins would tread a fine line between the violence intrinsic to the story and a PG-13 movie rating. If the film were rated R, her core audience of readers would be too young to see it in theaters. "The situations are so intense and frightening; it's just going to be a matter of creating suspense," Jacobson said. "The power of movies can be just as much about what you don't see as what you do."

In February 2011, Collins flew to Los Angeles, to meet with Ross and to begin collaborating on her draft of the script. "I think we had maybe fifteen minutes of discussion, and then we instantly transitioned into writing together seamlessly," Ross said, adding,

[She'd] pitch a line and I'd pitch the next line and before you knew it, we had a dialogue scene. And then we were both just getting excited from that. These are characters and a world that's entirely her invention. Sometimes we'll be working on a scene together and I almost get this giddy feeling because the characters we're talking about are the ones she's created.

Their screenwriting sessions continued long after midnight. Veteran screenwriter Billy Ray came on board to further develop the script. Collins and Ross also discussed movie sets, costumes, and casting decisions.

Fans of *The Hunger Games* had long imagined what the book's cast of characters looked like. Although seeing the book come to life thrilled many of them, others weren't so sure. Readers inundated Ross with letters. Students from one middle school in Texas sent him 150 letters alone. Worried that the movie wouldn't follow the book, they begged Ross to focus on the heart of the story, not just the action. They were especially concerned about who would play Katniss.

"I think that fans want Katniss to belong to them and I understand that," Jacobson said. "And I think that sometimes with people who have a strong other identity—as a celebrity or as a well-known other character—you feel like that person doesn't belong to you and I think that's what fans are looking for."

On March 17, 2011, after months of speculation, Collins announced in a press release, "Dear Readers. We have found Katniss." They had cast actress Jennifer Lawrence as Katniss. Lawrence played Mystique in the movie *X-Men: First Class* and received an Academy Award nomination for her role in *Winter's Bone*. Despite her film credits, readers weren't convinced. Collins's announcement immediately touched off heated debates. Fans argued that Lawrence was too old, too curvy, too blond and too pale, unlike painfully skinny Katniss who was portrayed in the book as having olive-colored skin and

black hair. "People feel very passionately that their take on the character is unique and correct," Ross said. However, he confidently defended his choice, assuring fans Lawrence would be made to look like Katniss, and calling it "the easiest casting decision I ever made in my life."

Jennifer Lawrence in 2011

Collins also tried to put her followers at ease. "I watched Jennifer embody every essential quality necessary to play Katniss," she said.

> I saw a girl who has the potential rage to send an arrow into the Gamemakers and the protectiveness to make Rue her ally. Who has conquered both Peeta and Gale's hearts even though she's done her best to wall herself off emotionally from anything that would lead to romance. Most of all, I believed that this was a girl who could hold out that handful of berries and incite the beaten down districts of Panem to rebel. I think that was the essential question for me. Could she believably inspire a rebellion? Did she project the strength, defiance, and intellect you would need to follow her into certain war? For me, she did.

The chance to play Katniss thrilled and worried Lawrence. "I know from the bottom of my heart that I love Katniss," she said.

> It's kind of like when you have a huge crush on somebody, and it's almost scary because you don't want to mess it up and have it not be everything you hope it will be. That's exactly what I feel about this. I'm terrified. Is it going to be good enough? Am I going to be good enough?

Josh Hutcherson in 2008

Ross and Collins soon announced more casting decisions. Josh Hutcherson captured the role of Peeta Mellark, the male tribute from Katniss's district. Hutcherson, who starred in *The Polar Express* and *The Bridge to Terabithia*, had read The Hunger Games series in five days. Collins strongly supported Hutcherson for the role of Peeta. "People may get thrown, say, by the color of an actor's hair, or something physical," she said. "But I tell you, if Josh had been bright purple and had six-foot wings and gave that audition, I'd have been like, 'Cast him! We can work around the wings.' He was that good."

Liam Hemsworth in 2011

Australian actor Liam Hemsworth was chosen for the role of Gale Hawthorne, Katniss's hunting companion. He and Hutcherson would become close friends off the set. Next, Ross and Collins cast Woody Harrelson as Haymitch, Katniss's and Peeta's drunk, but decent, coach; Lenny Kravitz as Katniss's gentle, talented stylist, Cinna; and Donald Sutherland as Panem's evil leader, President Snow.

Production began in May 2011, with the movie slated to open on March 23, 2012. Ross planned to film the movie in the western part of North Carolina, in a lush, green, mountainous area with more than 250 waterfalls. Most of the scenes of the Capitol would be filmed in the nearby city of Charlotte, where many of the actors stayed during production. The movie had a budget of approximately $80 million.

Movie hype contributed to the trilogy's continued rise in popularity. Sales of the three books soared, doubling from May to June 2011. At one library in North Carolina, all twenty-five copies of the books were checked out, with thirty-five people on the waiting lists. As word of mouth spread, many teachers added it to their students' summer reading lists. Kansas State University made it mandatory reading for incoming freshman.

Additional Hunger Games-themed merchandise appeared online and in stores. *The Hunger Games Companion*, a book by Lois Gresh, explored the real world social, political, economic, and psychological aspects of the trilogy. *The Hunger Games Tribute Guide* offered detailed profiles of all twenty-four tributes participating in the fight to the death. *The Unofficial Hunger Games Cookbook* featured recipes based on the book, such as lamb stew, apple-smoked groosling, and Capitol-grade dark chocolate cake. Fans purchased Hunger Games-related items ranging from t-shirts, posters, nail polish, socks, and jewelry to Katniss-style exercise workouts and Katniss-inspired Barbie dolls. People's interest in archery soared, as Katniss excels with a bow and arrow. Collins also worked with National Entertainment Collectibles Association and Striker Entertainment, a licensing agency, to create a line of merchandise, including board games, card games, collectibles, action figures, and bookmarks.

Jennifer Lawrence during filming
of the movie

Collins arrives at the world premiere of *The Hunger Games*.

Schools, libraries, and bookstores capitalized on the excitement over the movie's release and offered programs based on the trilogy. Schools held quiz bowls and read ins. At one school, students read *The Hunger Games* and fourteen other books, and then competed to answer trivia questions. Winning teams won tickets to see the movie on opening day. One principal read *The Hunger Games* for fifteen minutes each day over the school loudspeaker. Everyone—from custodians to teachers to students—followed along in their copies of the book. "They can't stop reading it," said high school librarian Sharon Nardelli. "Kids who never wanted to read are reading like crazy." Readers young and old attended book groups and costume contests in which they dressed like characters from the books.

After months of filming, sometimes under difficult conditions, the movie was ready. "The last day of shooting was more emotional than I have experienced on any movie," said Ross.

There was a strange feeling of catharsis and conclusion. The crew grew close, and it was very emotional for everyone. Maybe it was the extremity of what we had done—torrential rains, filming 100 feet up in the trees, lighting the woods on fire, etc. Maybe it was the story itself, but it was a very special time.

On February 22, 2012, a month before the movie's release, fans started buying tickets. They quickly set a record for advance ticket sales of a non-sequel movie. More than 2,000 show times for theaters across the United States sold out. The movie debuted at midnight on March 23 and became an instant hit. In the first weekend, it grossed an estimated $155 million at theaters in the United States and approximately $59 million overseas, a feat trumped only by *Harry Potter and the Deathly Hallows Part 2* and *The Dark Knight*. The film set a new record for the highest opening of a non-sequel movie in history. For three weeks, *The Hunger Games* movie remained in the number one spot, earning more than $460 million worldwide. It ranked among the biggest box office successes in history.

Lionsgate already had plans in the works to make movies of *Catching Fire* and *Mockingjay*. Although Ross called directing *The Hunger Games* "the happiest experience of my professional life," he made the choice not to work on *Catching Fire*. Due to the planned movie release of November 2013, Ross decided the tight production schedule wouldn't allow him time to write and make the movie he wanted. The search for a new director began immediately, with filming slated to begin in August 2012. Simon Beaufoy, the Academy Award-winning writer of *Slumdog Millionaire*, had already begun writing the screenplay for *Catching Fire*, and the original cast had signed on for the film. Lionsgate planned to split *Mockingjay* into two movies.

As fans continued to go to the theaters in droves, Collins shied away from any further attention. She preferred her privacy and concentrating on her writing. Despite the movie hype, many fans wondered what more Collins had in store for them.

Lawrence and Hemsworth as Katniss and Gale

Beyond Panem

The Hunger Games trilogy and smash hit movie brought Collins a level of fame most authors don't achieve in a lifetime. Her vivid futuristic world of Panem and her tough heroine Katniss captured the imaginations of readers on every continent except Antarctica, making The Hunger Games one of the best-selling young adult series in history.

With millions of copies in print, the books have topped best seller lists, and the trilogy is available in forty-one countries. *The Hunger Games* remained on the *New York Times* list for more than three consecutive years, and it ranks among the top ten most frequently borrowed library books in the country. And, it is the best-selling e-book ever for the Kindle reading device.

Collins and her books have captured numerous awards. Respected magazines and newspapers have praised each book in the trilogy, including naming them Top Ten Fiction Book of the Year, Best Book of the Year, Notable Book of the Year, and Best Children's Book of the Year. In 2010, *Time* magazine listed Collins as one of the year's most influential people, and *Entertainment Weekly* named her Entertainer of the Year.

Despite the multitude of fans, many people dislike Collins's books because of their violent content. According to the American Library Association, *The Hunger Games* was one of the most frequently challenged books in 2011, a feat the *Washington Post* called "a virtual rite of passage for young adult sensations." Complaints are varied: "anti-ethnic; anti-family; insensitivity; offensive language; occult/satanic; and violence." The criticism doesn't bother Collins, who carefully considers the level of violence that is essential to the story. "I've read in passing that people were concerned about the level of violence in the books," she said. "That's not unreasonable. They are violent. It's a war trilogy."

With the spotlight trained on The Hunger Games, often people overlook The Underland Chronicles, Collins's first best-selling series. Available in seven languages, more than 1 million copies of her books about Gregor the Overlander are in print.

Collins stands at the head of the young adult fantasy boom in publishing. Due to books like *Harry Potter and the Sorcerer's Stone*, *Twilight*, and *The*

The Harry Potter series became so popular that Universal Studios in Orlando built a model of Hogwarts Castle as part of the park.

Hunger Games, the popularity of fantasy has soared. It is the "golden age of fantasy for middle grade and young adult readers," according to Mallory Loehr, an editor-in-chief at Random House. More readers are taking home fantasy and science fiction books from libraries and bookstores, and enjoying series like Artemis Fowl, The Spiderwick Chronicles, and The Inheritance Trilogy. Because of the nature of the genre, the same stories often appeal to both children and adults. As with The Hunger Games, different aspects of the stories attract readers, who define the books in personal ways. Some enjoy the strange, futuristic worlds, others the action and adventure, and others the romance.

In turn, more authors are taking a stab at writing fantasy tales. Sharyn November, senior editor of Viking Children's Books, sees more publishers buying trilogies from authors in the United States, the United Kingdom, and Australia. "It is difficult today to find a publishing house without a fantasy title on its list," she said. "It's obvious that Harry Potter and the recent renewed focus on Lord of the Rings have done a lot to widen the awareness of fantasy in general, as well as of trilogies and series." In some ways, it represents a return to the past, as many classic children's stories, like *Alice in Wonderland* and *The Wizard of Oz*, are fantasies.

Despite Collins's success, and the authors she has inspired, Collins remains humble. When asked how she would spend $1 million, Collins said she would donate some to charity and save the rest, so that if everyone stopped buying her books, she could continue to be a writer. Collins prefers to live her life quietly, out of the limelight, and remains dedicated to crafting stories people want to read.

Part of Collins's brain has been in Panem continuously since 2007, when she first began penning the trilogy. While editing *The Hunger Games*, she worked on *Catching Fire*. Revisions of *Catching Fire* overlapped the writing of *Mockingjay*. She toured bookstores across the country, drafted the screenplay, and collaborated on *The Hunger Games* movie. Although Collins continues to concentrate primarily on The Hunger Games, she has seeds of ideas growing for other books. Collins is researching another young adult series and tossing around the notion of

writing an autobiographical children's book about
the year her father served overseas. She plans to use
her family members' names and base illustrations on
family photographs. "I specifically want to do this
book, one as sort of a memory piece kind of honoring that year for my family, and two, because I know
so many children are experiencing it right now—
having deployed parents," Collins said. "And it's a
way I would like to try and communicate my own
experience to them."

To Collins, one of her greatest achievements as
an author is writing books that have encouraged
more children to read. She said:

> One of the most memorable things I hear is
> when someone tells me that my books got
> a reluctant reader to read. They'll say, 'You
> know, there's this kid and he wouldn't touch
> a book and his parents found him under a
> blanket with a flashlight after bedtime be-
> cause he couldn't wait to find out what hap-
> pened in the next chapter.' That's just the
> best feeling. The idea that you might have
> contributed to a child's enjoyment of reading.

Recently, *The Hunger Games* played a role in
National Literacy Month. Lionsgate and Scholastic
paired with Scribd, the world's largest social reading
platform, with more than 75 millions readers each
month. Together, they created an app, or application,
that allowed people to read the first two chapters of

The Hunger Games on Scribd, Facebook, or Twitter and to share it with their friends. They also teamed up with DonorsChoose.org, a nonprofit organization, to create a contest. Anyone who used the app to read *The Hunger Games* would be entered into a sweepstakes to win a library of books for a classroom.

In 2012, *The Hunger Games* became one of thirty books chosen by librarians and booksellers as part of World Book Night. Other books included *The Book Thief*, *The Stand*, and *Because of Winn-Dixie*. Event planners organized thousands of volunteers to give away nearly 3 million books on April 23, 2012, the International Day of the Book. The date honors William Shakespeare and Miguel de Cervantes, who both died on April 23, 1616. On World Book Night, volunteers in the United States and Europe gave books away at locations ranging from prisons, baseball and

A volunteer gives books away on the Brighton to London train line as part of World Book Night.

soccer fields, hospitals, nursing homes, and food pantries. Printers, publishers, and paper companies volunteered to cover the costs of printing special paperback editions of the titles and the authors agreed to waive royalties they would have earned. Novelist Anna Quindlen said World Book Night is "like an intellectual Halloween, only better. We're giving out books, not just Mars bars." Through one person simply handing a book he or she loved to another person, the organizers of World Book Night hoped to improve literacy and to share a love of reading.

From a young age, Collins loved reading. The books she enjoyed as a child and has reread many times over the years inspire her writing. Aspects of *The Hunger Games* are drawn from some of her favorite fantasy classics: *Fahrenheit 451* by Ray Bradbury and *1984* by George Orwell. Like them, *The Hunger Games* presents a dystopian society, the opposite of a utopia, a perfect society. A dystopia is a bleak world in which people feel hopeless, frightened, and oppressed by the government. "Dystopian stories are places where you can play out the scenarios in your head—your anxieties—and see what might come of them," said Collins. Her books share key ingredients with *Fahrenheit 451* and *1984*—all are set in worlds ruled by harsh governments that abolish basic rights and control people through fear and each features a rebellious main character.

In *Fahrenheit 451*, Ray Bradbury told the tale of Guy Montag, a fireman living in a society that burns books. The elimination of books equals the elimination of free ideas and thought. The government, in which many have blind faith, censors information and feeds the people propaganda to the point that no one can distinguish fact from fiction. Intellectual freedom and individual liberties do not exist. However, when Montag attempts to break free, Bradbury's book ends with a small ray of hope for the future.

Moira Young, author of *Blood Red Road*, a book about a dystopian society, said:

> We create harsh, violent worlds. These are dark, sometimes bleak stories, but that doesn't mean they are hopeless. Those of us who write for young people are reluctant to leave our readers without hope. It wouldn't be right. We always leave a candle burning in the darkness.

George Orwell told a similar tale in his book *1984*. Set after a global war, the government of Oceania spies on citizens and punishes them severely for any indication of free will or speech. "Big Brother" serves as the figurehead of the ruling political party. The vast majority of citizens, called proles or proletariats, are kept impoverished, desperate for basic food and shelter. Winston Smith, the book's main character, eventually rebels. Today, the term Big Brother has come to symbolize governmental power, surveillance, and the collapse of civil liberties.

Often authors, like Collins, write books about dystopian societies because they see frightening trends in the real world. The stories have roots in reality, although they sometimes seem to be extreme warnings. To Collins, there is a distinct uneasiness in the country that kids feel today. Writing The Hunger Games

An advertisement for the film version of George Orwell's *1984*

trilogy wasn't just about telling a good story; she wanted the books to make children and adults think about the world in which they live.

Collins said, "You have to at some time in your life begin to question the environment, the political situation around you and decide, you know, whether it's right or not and if it isn't, what part you're going to play in that."

When Collins placed Katniss in Panem, a world in which hope is all but lost, she had in mind some of the problems people are facing now. Panem resembles countries in the world today, where repressive regimes erode civil liberties and punish citizens who invoke free speech. In early 2011, rebellions against such governments swept across countries in the Middle East, such as Tunisia, Egypt, Bahrain, and Libya. Just as people in Katniss's world ate pine-needle broth and entrail stew to survive, many people in the real world face severe hunger. Stricken by poverty, people in the Caribbean country of Haiti are resorting to eating "biscuits" made of sun-baked mud to fill their stomachs. The United Nations estimates that 925 million people worldwide suffer from extreme, life threatening hunger.

Collins doesn't shirk from showing reality, however harsh it may be. For her, it's important to write about war—its concept, nature, and ethics. Her books are variations of war stories, featuring prisoners of war, assassinations, biological weapons, genocide, and military intelligence. In the worlds Collins creates, she explores what is necessary and unnecessary about war. She wants her readers to consider questions about war, such as determining at what point armed rebellion becomes the only choice.

Inspired by her father, Collins believes in introducing difficult topics to children—the earlier the better—so they can hear about issues and understand them without being scared. To Collins, many subjects aren't talked about the way they should be, because they're uncomfortable and unpleasant to discuss. Collins hopes that earlier dialogue about war and other complex issues will help lead to more solutions.

She said:

> Obviously, we're not in a position at the moment for the eradication of war to seem like anything but a far-off dream. But at one time, the eradication of slave markets in the United States seemed very far off. I mean, people have to begin somewhere. We can change. We can evolve as a species. It's not simple, and it's a very long and drawn-out process, but you can hope.

Collins also worries that the line between reality and reality television is blurring as people are exposed to images in movies, on television, and on the Internet. With hundreds of channels and countless Web sites, news programming no longer stands out as different from other stories on television.

She said:

Very young children don't even have the capacity to distinguish. But as kids get older, you have to sit down with them . . . and say, 'You know, this is a game, this is made up,' and . . . 'This is news footage, this really happened,' so that children understand someone getting voted off a show is not the same thing as a tsunami . . . they have to know that it's not just stuff that happens in this box and it's contained and you can turn it on and off. That there's real life occurring that doesn't end when the commercials roll.

The Hunger Games trilogy gives readers much to ponder—hunger, poverty, war, rebellion, governmental power, freedom of speech, and decision making. Collins's books are stories of honor and courage at the worst of times. They carry a strong antiviolence message that rings true with readers young and old.

It is Collins's younger readers who she especially hopes will look beyond the romance and action in her books to the deeper issues within the story. To Collins, it is those young adults who can one day make a difference in the world. She adds:

It's crucial that young readers are considering scenarios about humanity's future, because the challenges are about to land in their laps. I hope they question how elements of the books might be relevant in their own lives. About global warming, about our mistreatment of the environment, but also questions like: How do you feel about the fact that some people take their next meal for granted when so many other people are starving in the world? What do you think about choices your government, past and present, or other governments around the world make? What's your relationship to reality TV versus your relationship to the news? Was there anything in the book that disturbed you because it reflected aspects of your own life, and if there was, what can you do about it? Because you know what? Even if they're not of your making, these issues and how to deal with them will become your responsibility.

TIMELINE

1962	Born August 10 in Hartford, Connecticut.
1968	Moves to Indiana; father serves in Vietnam War.
1973	Moves with family to Brussels, Belgium.
1980	Graduates from Alabama School of Fine Arts; enters Indiana University where she marries Cap Pryor.
1985	Graduates from Indiana University with degrees in Telecommunications and Theater and Drama.
1987	Moves to New York City; begins studying screenwriting at New York University.
1991	Starts career in television writing, leading to work on multiple children's shows.
1994	Son, Charlie, born.
1999	Daughter, Isabel, born.
2003	Moves to Connecticut; publishes *Gregor the Overlander,* the first in a five-book best-selling series.
2004	Publishes *Gregor and the Prophecy of Bane.*
2005	Publishes *Gregor and the Curse of the Warmbloods* and *When Charlie McButton Lost Power.*
2006	Publishes *Gregor and the Marks of Secret.*
2007	Publishes *Gregor and the Code of Claw.*
2008	Publishes *The Hunger Games*; tops *New York Times* bestseller list for 180 consecutive weeks; receives more than seventy awards.
2009	Publishes *Catching Fire*; Lionsgate acquires movie rights to *The Hunger Games.*
2010	Publishes *Mockingjay,* debuting at number one spot on multiple best seller lists; named to the *Time* 100 list.
2012	Release of *The Hunger Games* movie; sets records for ticket sales; becomes best-selling e-book author in history; has more than 36 million copies of trilogy in print.

SOURCES

CHAPTER 1 A Soldier's Daughter

p. 11, "fairy-tale magical . . ." Susan Dominus, "Suzanne Collins's War Stories for Kids," *New York Times*, April 8, 2011, http://www.nytimes.com.

p. 14, "If your parent . . ." Dominus, "Suzanne Collins's War Stories for Kids."

p. 16, "I believe he felt . . ." Hillel Italie, "How Has 'Hunger Games' Author Suzanne Collins's Life Changed?"*Huffington Post*, September 23, 2010, http://www.huffingtonpost.com.

p. 18, "And this was . . ." Dominus, "Suzanne Collins's War Stories for Kids."

p. 19, "I think it's important . . ." "Suzanne Collins Answers Questions About the Hunger Games Trilogy," YouTube video, 3:08, http://www.youtube.com/watch?v=FH15DI8ZW14.

p. 20, "Even when I . . ." Melissa Block, "Edgy Violent Thrillers for the Teen-Age set," NPR, September 1, 2009, http://www.npr.org.

CHAPTER 2 From Acting to Writing

p. 24, "We like the . . ." Eric Berman, "Forest Game Will Open Tonight," *Indiana Daily Student*, December 3, 1984.

p. 25, "They always allowed . . ." "Author Interviews," Scholastic video, 8:20, from an interview in June 2008, http://www.scholastic.com/browse/video.

p. 29, "I find there isn't . . ." "Author Profile: Suzanne Collins," *Teen Reads*, August 2010, http://www.teenreads.com.

p. 35, "She seemed like . . ." Italie, "How Has 'Hunger Games' Author Suzanne Collins's Life Changed?"

CHAPTER 3 Creating the Underland

p. 38, "very dramatic . . ." Susan Carpenter, "Catching Fire Could Prompt a Literary Hunger," *Los Angeles Times*, September 2, 2009, http://www.latimes.com.

p. 39, "I liked the fact . . ." http://www.suzannecollinsbooks.com.

p. 41, "I love bats . . ." Ibid.

p. 42, "I think I'm like . . ." Ibid.

p. 42, "The rest of . . ." "Author Profile: Suzanne Collins."

p. 43, "In a book . . ." Rick Margolis, "The Last Battle: With Mockingjay on the Way, Suzanne Collins Weighs In on Katniss and the Capitol," *School Library Journal*, August 1, 2010, http://www.schoollibraryjournal.com.

p. 43,   "Quite honestly . . ." Italie, "How Has 'Hunger Games' Author Suzanne Collins's Life Changed?"

p. 47,   "Somewhere along the way . . ." Carpenter, "Catching Fire Could Prompt a Literary Hunger."

CHAPTER 4 *The Hunger Games*

p. 49,   "I was attracted . . ." Karen Springen, "This Isn't Child's Play," *Daily Beast*, September 4, 2008, http://www.thedailybeast.com.

p. 54,   "In a way . . ." "Five Questions with Suzanne Collins: Author of The Hunger Games Trilogy," YouTube video, 2:43, http://www.youtube.com/watch?v=twCq84Bm-_8.

p. 55,   "When you're going . . ." Rick Margolis, "A Killer Story," *School Library Journal*, September 2008, http://www.schoollibraryjournal.com.

p. 55,   "It's an enormous . . ." Ibid.

p. 56,   "Although set in . . ." Kate Egan, *The Hunger Game: The Official Illustrated Movie Companion* (New York, Scholastic Press, 2012), 9.

p. 56,   "I remember that . . ." Ibid., 10.

pp. 58-59,"It's one of those . . ." Thomas Pardee, "The Hunger Games," *Advertising Age*, November 15, 2010, http://www.adage.com.

p. 59,   "Once I'd thought . . ." Jorge Carreon, "Literary Youthquake: A Q&A with Author Suzanne Collins and *The Hunger Games*," *Examiner*, January 6, 2009, http://www.examiner.com.

p. 60,   "Catching Fire . . ." "Books of Note," Scholastic, http://www.mediaroom. scholastic.com/hungergames.

p. 61,   "You sort of . . ." Elissa Petruzzi, "To the Death: Suzanne Collins Kills," *RT Book Reviews*, September 2009, http://www.rtbookreviews.com.

p. 62,   "No! . . ." Dominus, "Suzanne Collins's War Stories for Kids."

p. 62,   "I've never . . ." Diane Roback, "Children's Fiction Bestsellers," *Publishers Weekly*, August 9, 2010, http://www.publishersweekly.com.

p. 64,   "At the risk of . . ." "Teen Alert: Mockingjay Arrives Early Tuesday," *USA Today*, August 19, 2010, http://www.usatoday.com.

p. 64,   "After months of anticipation . . ." "*Mockingjay*, the Final Book in The Hunger Games Trilogy by Suzanne Collins Tops All National Bestseller Lists with Sales of More than 450,000 Copies in its First Week of Publication," Scholastic, http://www.mediaroom.scholastic.com/hungergames.

p. 65,   "A visit from . . ." "Powell's Books in Portland, Oregon Wins Scholastic Bookstore Contest Prize of Store Visit by Suzanne Collins, Bestselling Author of The Hunger Games Trilogy," Scholastic, http://www. mediaroom.scholastic.com/hungergames.

CHAPTER 5 The Big Screen

p. 68,   "I just picked . . ." Egan, *The Hunger Game: The Official Illustrated Movie Companion*, 12.

p. 68,   "I became . . ." Ibid., 13.

p. 68,   "Lionsgate is known . . ." Ibid.

p. 69,   "I mentioned . . ." Ibid., 15.

p. 70,   "I felt very . . ." Karen Valby, "Hunger Games Exclusive: Why Gary Ross Got the Coveted Job, and Who Suggested Megan Fox for the Lead Role," *Entertainment Weekly*, January 6, 2011, http://www.insidemovies.ew.com.

p. 70,   "The situations are . . ." Denise Martin, "The Next Twilight," *Daily Beast*, August 28, 2010, http://www.thedailybeast.com.

pp. 70-71,"I think we had . . ." Karen Valby, "Team Hunger Games Talks: Author Suzanne Collins and Director Gary Ross on Their Allegiance to Each Other and Their Actors," *Entertainment Weekly*, April 7, 2011, http://www.ew.com.

p. 71,   "I think that . . ." Valby, "Hunger Games Exclusive: Why Gary Ross Got the Coveted Job, and Who Suggested Megan Fox for the Lead Role."

p. 72,   "People feel very . . ." Karen Valby, "Games Gets Its Girl," *Entertainment Weekly*, April 1, 2011, http://www.ew.com.

p. 73,   "I watched Jennifer . . ." Darren Franich, "Hunger Games: Suzanne Collins Talks Jennifer Lawrence as Katniss," *Entertainment Weekly*, March 21, 2011, http://www.ew.com.

p. 73,   "I know from . . ." Karen Valby, "The Chosen One," *Entertainment Weekly*, May 27, 2011, http://www.ew.com.

p. 74,   "People may get . . ." Karen Valby, "Brave Hearts," *Entertainment Weekly*, August 5, 2011, http://www.ew.com.

p. 81,   "They can't stop . . ." Lauren Barack, "Librarians Hope to Build Readers on Hunger Games Excitement," *School Library Journal*, February 21, 2012.

p. 81,   "The last day . . ." Egan, *The Hunger Games: The Official Illustrated Movie Companion*,150.

p. 82,   "the happiest experience of my professional life." Sophie Haslett, "Gary Ross Will Not Direct *The Hunger Games* Sequel," *Telegraph*, April 11, 2012, http://www.telegraph.co.uk.

CHAPTER 6 Beyond Panem

p. 86, "a virtual rite . . ." "Ten Most Frequently Challenged Books of 2010," *Christian Science Monitor*, April 12, 2011, http://www.csmonitor.com.

p. 86, "anti-ethnic . . ." Stephan Lee, "*The Hunger Games* Ignites the ALA's List of Most Challenged Books," April 9, 2012, http://www.ew.com.

p. 86, "I've read in passing . . ." "Ten Most Frequently Challenged Books of 2010."

p. 87, "golden age . . ." Sally Lodge, "Beyond the Wizard's Wand," *Publishers Weekly*, June 30, 2003, http://www.publishersweekly.com.

p. 88, "It is difficult . . ." Ibid.

p. 89, "I specifically want . . ." Dominus, "Suzanne Collins's War Stories for Kids."

p. 89, "One of the most . . ." Hannah Trierweiler Hudson, "Sit Down with Suzanne Collins," *Instructor*, Fall 2010.

p. 91, "like an intellectual . . ." Bob Minzesheimer, "World Book Night Celebrates Reading with Paperback Handouts," *USA Today*, April 23, 2012, http://www.usatoday.com.

p. 91, "Dystopian stories . . ." Italie, 'How Has 'Hunger Games' Author Suzanne Collins's Life Changed?'

p. 92, "We create . . ." Moira Young, "Why is Dystopia So Appealing to Young Adults?" *Observer*, October 22, 2011, http://www.guardian.co.uk.

p. 94, "You have to at some time . . ." Block, "Edgy Violent Thrillers for the Teen-Age Set."

p. 95, "Obviously, we're not . . ." Rick Margolis, "The Last Battle," *School Library Journal*, August 1, 2010, http://www.schoollibraryjournal.com.

p. 96, "Very young children . . ." Hannah Trierweiler Hudson, "Sit Down with Suzanne Collins."

p. 98, "It's crucial that . . ." Egan, *The Hunger Games: The Official Illustrated Movie Companion*, 158.

BIBLIOGRAPHY

Alabama School of Fine Arts official Web site. http://www.asfa.k12.al.us.

"Author Interviews." Scholastic video, 8:20, from an interview in June 2008. http://www.scholastic.com/browse/video.

"Author Profile: Suzanne Collins." *Teen Reads*, August 2010. http://www.teenreads.com.

Barack, Lauren. "Librarians Hope to Build Readers on Hunger Games Excitement." *School Library Journal*, February 21, 2012.

Berman, Eric. "Forest Game Will Open Tonight." *Indiana Daily Student*, December 3, 1984.

Bethune, Brian. "Do Not Open Until August 24." *Maclean's*, August 30, 2010. http://www.macleans.ca.

Block, Melissa. "Edgy, Violent Thrillers for the Teen-Age Set." NPR, September 1, 2009. http://www.npr.org.

Carpenter, Susan. "Catching Fire Could Prompt a Literary Hunger." *Los Angeles Times*, September 2, 2009. http://www.latimes.com.

Cassani, Kerrie. "Hollywood Hungry for North Carolina Mountain Climate." *The Weather Channel*, March 18, 2012. http://www.weather.com.

Carreon, Jorge. "Literary Youthquake: A Q&A with Author Suzanne Collins and *The Hunger Games*." *Examiner*, January 6, 2009. http://www.examiner.com.

Child, Ben. "The Hunger Games' Katniss Gets the Barbie Doll Treatment." *Guardian*, March 26, 2012. http://www.guardian.co.uk.

Coleman, Miriam. "'The Hunger Games' Breaks Box Office Records for Opening Weekend." *Rolling Stone*, March 26, 2012. http://www.rollingstone.com.

Collins, Suzanne. *Gregor the Overlander*. New York: Scholastic, 2003.

———. *The Hunger Games*. New York: Scholastic, 2008.

Dominus, Susan. "Suzanne Collins's War Stories for Kids." *New York Times*, April 8, 2011. http://www.nytimes.com.

Egan, Kate. *The Hunger Games: The Official Illustrated Movie Companion*. New York, Scholastic Press, 2012.

"Five Questions with Suzanne Collins: Author of The Hunger Games Trilogy," YouTube video, 2:43, http://www.youtube.com/watch?v=twCq84Bm-_8.

Franich, Darren. "Hunger Games: Suzanne Collins Talks Jennifer Lawrence as Katniss." *Entertainment Weekly*, March 21, 2011. http://www.ew.com.

Gresh, Lois H. *The Hunger Games Companion*. New York: St. Martin's Griffin, 2011.

Gundell, Sara. *Suzanne Collins: Fame*. Vancouver, WA: Bluewater Productions, 2012.

Haslett, Sophie. "Gary Ross Will Not Direct *The Hunger Games* Sequel." *Telegraph*, April 11, 2012. http://www.telegraph.co.uk.

Hopkinson, Deborah. "A Riveting Return to the World of *The Hunger Games*." *BookPage*, September 2009. http://www.bookpage.com.

Horn, Lyndsey. "Greenville Fans Eat Up 'The Hunger Games.'" *Daily Reflector*, March 26, 2012. http://www.reflector.com.

Hudson, Hannah Trierweiler. "Sit Down with Suzanne Collins." *Instructor*, Fall 2010.

Indiana University official Web site. http://www.indiana.edu.

Italie, Hillel. "How Has 'Hunger Games' Author Suzanne Collins's Life Changed?" *Huffington Post*, September 23, 2010. http://www.huffingtonpost.com.

Jordan, Tina. "Suzanne Collins on the Books She Loves." *Entertainment Weekly*, August 12, 2010. http://www.ew.com.

Lee, Stephan. "*The Hunger Games* Ignites the ALA's List of the Most Challenged Books." *Entertainment Weekly*, April 9, 2012. http://www.ew.com.

"Let the Games Continue." *USA Today*, September 1, 2009. http://www.usatoday.com.

Lodge, Sally. "Beyond the Wizard's Wand." *Publishers Weekly*, June 30, 2003. http://www.publishersweekly.com.

Margolis, Rick. "A Killer Story." *School Library Journal*, September 2008. http://www.schoollibraryjournal.com.

———. "The Last Battle." *School Library Journal*, August 1, 2010. http://www.schoollibraryjournal.com.

Martin, Denise. "The Next Twilight." *Daily Beast*, August 28, 2010. http://www.thedailybeast.com.

Minzesheimer, Bob. "World Book Night Celebrates Reading with Paperback Handouts." *USA Today*, April 23, 2012. http://www.usatoday.com.

New York University official Web site. http://www.nyu.edu.

Pardee, Thomas. "The Hunger Games." *Advertising Age*, November 15, 2010. http://www.adage.com.

Petruzzi, Elissa. "To the Death: Suzanne Collins Kills." *RT Book Reviews*, September 2009. http://www.rtbookreviews.com.

Roback, Diane. "Children's Fiction Bestsellers." *Publishers Weekly*, August 9, 2010. http://www.publishersweekly.com.

Scholastic official Web site. http://www.mediaroom.scholastic.com.

Sellers, John A. "A Dark Horse Breaks Out." *Publishers Weekly*, June 9, 2008. http://www.publishersweekly.com.

———. "Hungry? The Latest on *The Hunger Games*." *Publishers Weekly*, March 12, 2009. http://www.publishersweekly.com.

Springen, Karen. "This Isn't Child's Play." *Daily Beast*, September 4, 2008. http://www.thedailybeast.com.

Sullivan, Kevin P. "Hunger Games Shoots Down All-Time Records." MTV, April 9, 2012. http://www.mtv.com.

"Suzanne Collins Answers Questions About the Hunger Games Trilogy," YouTube video, 3:08. http://www.youtube.com/watch?v=FH15DI8ZW14.

Suzanne Collins official Web site. http://www.suzannecollinsbooks.com.

"Teen Alert: Mockingjay Arrives Early Tuesday." *USA Today*, August 19, 2010. http://www.usatoday.com.

"Ten Most Frequently Challenged Books of 2010." *Christian Science Monitor*, April 12, 2011. http://www.csmonitor.com.

The Hunger Games movie official Web site. http://www.thehungergamesmovie.com.

Tisch School of the Arts official Web site. http://tisch.nyu.edu.

Valby, Karen. "Brave Hearts." *Entertainment Weekly*, August 5, 2011. http://www.ew.com.

——. "Games Gets Its Girl." *Entertainment Weekly*, April 1, 2011. http://www.ew.com.

——. "Hunger Games Exclusive: Why Gary Ross Got the Coveted Job, and Who Suggested Megan Fox for the Lead Role." *Entertainment Weekly*, January 6, 2011. http://www.insidemovies.ew.com.

——. "Let the Hunger Games Begin." *Entertainment Weekly*, January 14, 2011. http://www.ew.com.

——. "Team Hunger Games Talks: Author Suzanne Collins and Director Gary Ross on Their Allegiance to Each Other and Their Actors." *Entertainment Weekly*, April 7, 2011. http://www.ew.com.

——. "The Chosen One." *Entertainment Weekly*, May 27, 2011. http://www.ew.com.

——. "*The Hunger Games* Nabs Two More Stars." *Entertainment Weekly*, April 15, 2011. http://www.ew.com.

Wilson, Leah. *The Girl Who Was On Fire*. Dallas, Texas: BenBella Books, Inc., 2010.

Young, Moira. "Why is Dystopia So Appealing to Young Adults?" *Observer*, October 22, 2011. http://www.guardian.co.uk.

WEB SITES

http://www.suzannecollinsbooks.com

Suzanne Collins's official Web site features descriptions and reviews of Collins's books, along with an interview and biography.

http://www.mediaroom.scholastic.com/hungergames

This is the official Web site of Scholastic. It offers a wealth of information including press releases, a list of awards, and links to interviews and news articles about Suzanne Collins and her work.

http://www.thehungergamesmovie.com

Readers interested in learning more about *The Hunger Games* movie can find information at this site, as well as news, photographs, posters, and information about the cast and crew.

INDEX

PHOTO CREDITS

All images used in this book that are not in the public domain are credited in the listing that follows:

Cover: Associated Press
6: Associated Press
12-13: Courtesy of the U.S. Army
15: Courtesy of Library of Congress
16-17: Courtesy of Myrabella
26-27: Courtesy of David Shankbone
31: Courtesy of NASA Goddard Space Flight Center
33: Courtesy of Jorge Barrios
34-35: Courtesy of Dougtone
44-45: Courtesy of Ed Morgan
47: Courtesy of Ed Morgan
52: Courtesy of aimmyarrowshigh
53: Courtesy of TeunSpaans
54: Courtesy of Ninjatacoshell
58, top right: Associated Press
58, bottom left: Associated Press
60: ZUMA Wire Service / Alamy
63: Copyright Michael Hurcomb/Corbis / APImages
69: Associated Press
72: Associated Press
74: Associated Press
75: Associated Press
76-77: Associated Press
78-79: Pictorial Press Ltd / Alamy
80-81: Associated Press
82-83: Associated Press
87: Courtesy of Carlos Cruz
90: Simon Dack / Alamy
93: Pictorial Press Ltd / Alamy
96-97: Courtesy of Dean (leu)